GW00994455

NEW LIFE

in the Spirit

a guidebook for the
Life in the Spirit Seminars

SERVANT
BOOKS

PUBLISHED BY ST. ANTHONY MESSENGER PRESS
CINCINNATI, OHIO

Nihil Obstat: Lawrence A. Gollner
                               Censor librorum

Imprimatur: Leo A. Pursley, D.D.
                               Bishop of Fort Wayne—South Bend

Book redesign by Phillips Robinette, O.F.M.

ISBN 0-89283-001-8

Published by Servant Books,
an imprint of St. Anthony Messenger Press
28 W. Liberty Street
Cincinnati, OH 45202
www.ServantBooks.org

Printed on acid-free paper

Printed in the United States of America

"To the thirsty I will give water without price from the fountain of the water of life…"

(Rev 21:6, RSV)

*This promise is for you, for you who want
    something more
For you who know that you have a thirst that
    has not yet been satisfied
For you who have heard of water that
    refreshes beyond compare
For you who feel burdened, who feel that you
    have reached the depths and want to rise
For you who are on top of the world, but who
    know that all the world does not have enough*

*For you who are full of fears and anxieties, for
you who feel hardened and closed
For you who are full of eagerness and
enthusiasm, for you who want all a human
being can have*

For all men, there is a promise, a promise made
by your God, by the one who made you.

Perhaps you know him and have wondered if
there should not be more. Perhaps you have only
dimly heard of him and wish you could find him.

Now he speaks to you. Now he offers you a
promise, a free gift, a new life—without price. He
offers it to you freely, just as he created you
freely, because he loves you.

**"Let him who is thirsty come; let him who
desires take the water of life without price."
(Rev 22:17, RSV)**

Introduction

This book is a guideline, a companion. It will help you to find your way through the Life in the Spirit Seminars and to discover all the wealth that God wants to give you through them. This book will help you to find a deeper life in God.

God speaks to us and helps us through others. If you want new life in the Spirit, you should be faithful in attending the seminars, so that brothers and sisters can help you during them. God also speaks to us when we are alone, and he will do much for us when we are alone that cannot happen if we do not spend time with him. Spend time with God during these next seven weeks, and you will see him give you new life through that time.

Prayer

Prayer is simply being present with God. Our prayer can take a variety of forms: praising and worshipping him for his own sake; thanking him for what he has done for us; asking him to do things for us or for others; listening to him speak to us. Sometimes it is simply being quiet before him, silent in his presence.

Prayer will grow in you. At first, if it is new to you, it may go slowly. But as you come to know God more fully and experience his love, your desire to pray will increase. After you have been baptized in the Spirit, you will be able to pray still more freely. God wants you to pray because he loves you and wants you to be with him. He wants to give you the gift of prayer.

The words of life in this book will help you to pray. They are the words that God has spoken in the Scriptures. He means to speak them to you now. There is one for each day of the seven weeks of the seminars, and they are chosen to help you consider more deeply the material presented in the seminar the week before. Meditate on them each day in the time you have set aside for prayer, and the Lord will speak to you through them.

Study

True wisdom and true understanding are a gift from God. God himself wants to teach you. If you read the Scriptures, and if you think about what they say, asking the Lord to teach you, you will be given spiritual understanding.

For each week of the seminars, two chapters from Scripture are presented. They are chosen to prepare you for the seminar of the coming week. Each week one chapter will be from the good news according to John (the Gospel of John), and the other will be from the Acts of the Apostles or from a letter of the apostle Paul. Read these chapters and think about them during the week. If you can do more reading during the next seven weeks, read the full Gospel of John and the full Acts of the Apostles.

We have never failed to pray for you, and what we ask God is that through perfect wisdom and spiritual understanding you shall reach the fullest knowledge of his will. So you will be able to lead the kind of life which the Lord expects of you, a life acceptable to him in all its aspects; showing the results in all good actions you do and increasing your knowledge of God. You will have in you the strength, based on his own glorious power, never to give in, but to bear anything joyfully, thanking the Father who has made it possible for you to join the saints and with them to inherit the light.

(Col 1:9–12, JB)

GOD'S LOVE

"For God so loved the world that he gave his only Son, that whoever believes in him should not perish but have eternal life."
(Jn 3:16, RSV)

Words of Life

Day 1:

God is not someone who lives far away in a place you can never reach. Nor is he a heavenly warden, eager to punish you for doing wrong. He is a father who loves you. He says to you:

I have loved you with an everlasting love,
so I am constant in my affection for you.

(Jer 31:3, JB)

Day 2:

You can know God and know how much he loves you. He wants to be in a personal relationship with you. He wants you to be his son or daughter. He does not want there to be any barrier or distance between you and him. He promised through the prophet Jeremiah:

> *I will be their God and they shall be my people. There will be no further need for neighbor to try to teach neighbor, or brother to say to brother, "Learn to know the Lord!" No, they will all know me, the least no less than the greatest—it is the Lord who speaks—since I will forgive their iniquity and never call their sin to mind.*
>
> (adapted from Jer 31:33–34, JB)

This word of life is a promise, an offer from God. As soon as you feel that you want to take the Lord up on what he is offering in these words of life and receive what he is promising, read the section entitled, "God's Covenant" beginning on p. 14.

Day 3:

He loves you. God, the creator of the universe, the one who made all things out of nothing, loves you. He wants to care for you and give you a better life. He promised:

> *I myself will pasture my sheep, I myself will show them where to rest—it is the Lord God who speaks. I shall look for the lost one, bring back the stray, bandage the wounded and make the weak strong. I shall watch over the fat and healthy. I shall be a true shepherd to them.*
> (adapted from Ezek 34:14–16, JB)

Day 4:
Because he loves us, God sent his only son to save us. He sent Jesus so that we might have life, a better life now, a life that will last eternally.

> *For God so loved the world that he gave his only Son, that whoever believes in him should not perish but have eternal life.*
> (Jn 3:16, RSV)

Day 5:
God loves you. He is speaking to you now, reaching out to you. He is saying to you:

> *Oh, come to the water all you who are thirsty; though you have no money, come!...*

Why spend money on what is not bread,
your wages on what fails to satisfy?
Listen, listen to me, and you will have good
things to eat and rich food to enjoy.
Pay attention, come to me; listen, and your soul
will live.
With you I will make an everlasting covenant.

(Is 55:1–3, JB)

Day 6:

If you wish to know God, if you wish to have the life he offers, you can. Just turn to him and reach out to him. He invites you:

I know the plans I have in mind for you—it is the Lord who speaks—plans for peace, not disaster, reserving a future full of hope for you. Then when you call to me, and come to plead with me, I will listen to you. When you seek me, you shall find me.

(adapted from Jer 29:11–13, JB)

Day 7:

Sometimes God seems so far away. Sometimes it seems like we can never reach him. But he is not far away. He is very close to you, and right now he is trying to show himself to you in a fuller way than ever before. He promises:

> The LORD is near to all who call upon him,
> to all who call upon him in truth.
>
> (Ps 145:18, RSV)

Study

This week, the two chapters we will read are concerned with who Jesus Christ is and how he saves us. They are:

John 1, Colossians 1

GOD'S COVENANT

We can know that God is willing to have a personal relationship with us and to give us a new life only because he has told us so. He made many promises to us, and we can rely on the promises of God. He has all power in heaven and on earth, and he does not lie. He can do what he says and he will. But he will not force these things on us. We have to claim what he is offering. We have to believe what he says and receive from him what he wants to give.

Many of the "words of life" above are promises. We can claim these promises and hold God to them. We can base our lives upon them.

Your Covenant
God's gift of new life with him is free, absolutely free. We cannot earn it or deserve it in any way.

Yet, we have to receive what he is offering. We have to come to him and reach out to him.

A covenant is an agreement. When we enter into a covenant with someone, we make an agreement with that person. We can enter into a covenant with God because he has already offered a covenant to us. He has made us a promise that we can accept and claim.

If you make a covenant with God now for the period of the next seven weeks, you will find that you will have a new life with God at the end of that time.

God promises in the words of life above that if we turn to him and reach out for what he has to offer, he will give it to us. The covenant you should make with God is simply a covenant to turn to him, to listen to him, and to let other Christians help you.

Perhaps you already know God and have experienced his love. Perhaps what you are looking for is a deeper relationship with him, a fullness of life in his Spirit. If you enter into a covenant with him now in the same way and agree to seek from him what he is offering, he will give you that deeper life with him. You should agree to do those things which will allow God to give you the gift he has for you. For everyone in the seminars, those things are:

1) to attend and participate in the Life in the Spirit Seminars each week, without missing any of them

2) to set aside at least 15 minutes a day for prayer and study, meditating on the words of life in this book and studying the passages in the book (15 good minutes, not 15 minutes in which you are distracted)

3) to come each week to pray with the prayer group or community that is helping you find a new life in the Spirit

4) to share with others in the seminars each week how you are growing and what difficulties you are having

To make this covenant with God, say the following prayer:

Father, I want to find a new relationship with you and the new life you are promising. I want to know you more fully. I want to have you change my life and give me the power to live in a better way. To allow you to do this, I promise to attend the Life in the Spirit Seminars each week, to set aside 15 minutes each day to seek you on my own, to pray with the community each week, and to share with the others in the seminar how I am growing and what difficulties I am experiencing. I wish to allow you the chance to give me those things you have promised.

If you fail...

Remember that God loves you and wants you to be with him even more than you want him. He is not legalistic with us. If something happens so that we cannot fulfill our covenant one day, he will not hold it against us. If we neglect what we have promised, we can ask his forgiveness, and he will forgive us. He loves us and does not want anything to be a barrier between us and him. Of course, if we make a covenant with him, we should only do it because we want to and because we intend to fulfill our part of it. A covenant is a way of entering into a relationship of committed love with God.

"I have not
said,
'Seek me
in vain.'"

SALVATION

"He has taken us out of the power of darkness and created a place for us in the kingdom of the Son that he loves, and in him, we gain our freedom, the forgiveness of our sins."

(Col 1:13–14, JB)

Words of Life

Day 1:

We find ourselves in a world that has something seriously wrong with it. Daily we read about wars, murders, poverty, racial conflict, exploitation. Daily we see in others and in ourselves lone-liness, depression, anxiety, boredom, suspicion, mistrust, quarreling, hatred. Yet God did not create the world to be this way, nor does he want to be this way. He promised:

> In the days to come...the peoples will stream to [the temple of the Lord], nations without number will come to it; and they will say, "Come, let us go up to the mountain of the Lord...so that he may teach us his ways and we may walk in his paths...." He will wield authority over many peoples and arbitrate for mighty nations; they will hammer their swords into plowshares, their spears into sickles. Nations will not lift sword against nation, there will be no more training for war.... That day—it is the Lord who speaks—I will finally gather in the lame, and bring together those who have been led astray.

(adapted from Mic 4:1–6, JB)

Day 2:

Many men offer to us plans for making the world a better place. Better education, more technical skills, new political programs, sociological wisdom, drugs, are all offered as solutions. Man-made religions (Buddhism, Baha'i, Zen, yoga, and many others) are presented to us as the hope of the world. Some even tell us that a

Christian moral code without Christ is the solution. But all these are human thoughts, man-made plans. The Lord says:

> Yes, the heavens are as high above the earth
> as my ways are above your ways,
> my thoughts above your thoughts.

(Is 55:9, JB)

Day 3:

We need more than human ideas and human power. We need the wisdom and power of God. We are facing a power that is greater than human power. Behind the world's evils is an evil intelligence, a kingdom of evil spirits, something greater than we are. Each of us has sensed what Paul tells us:

> For it is not against human enemies that we have to struggle, but against the Sovereignties and the Powers who originate the darkness in this world, the spiritual army of evil in the heavens.

(Eph 6:12, JB)

Day 4:

God's answer to the world's need is Jesus Christ. Jesus was sent to this world to save us, to free us from the power of Satan and of the world, so that we might live a new life now and forevermore.

> Martha said to Jesus, "If you had been here, my brother would not have died, but I know that, even now whatever you ask of God, he will grant you...." Jesus said, "I am the resurrection. If anyone believes in me, even if he dies he will live, and whoever lives and believes in me will never die. Do you believe this?" "Yes, Lord," she said, "I believe that you are the Christ, the Son of God, the one who was to come into this world."
>
> (Jn 11:21–27, JB)

Day 5:

Our freedom costs something. Jesus had to die so that we might live. But God loved us enough to send his son, who willingly died for us. As Paul says:

> It is not easy to die even for a good man— though of course for someone really worthy, a man might be prepared to die—but what

proves that God loves us is that Christ died for
us while we were still sinners.

(Rom 5:6–8, JB)

Day 6:

Jesus died and rose from the dead so that we might have new life. If he had not died, if he had not undergone the sufferings he did, we could not have been freed from sin and from the power of Satan. The prophet Isaiah spoke of Christ:

Ours were the sufferings he bore, ours the sorrows he carried.... He was pierced through for our faults, crushed for our sins. On him lies a punishment that brings us peace, and through his wounds we are healed. We had all gone astray like sheep, each taking his own way, and the Lord burdened him with the sins of all of us.

(adapted from Is 53:4–6, JB)

Day 7:

When Jesus rose from the dead, he had defeated the power of Satan. Now he can free you from the power of darkness and the hold of

Satan's kingdom. He can give you a whole new life, if you are willing to leave the old.

> *He has taken us out of the power of darkness*
> *and created a place for us in the kingdom of the*
> *Son that he loves, and in him, we gain our*
> *freedom, the forgiveness of our sins.*
>
> (Col 1:13–14, JB)

Study

This week we will study the new life Jesus brings and the gift of the Holy Spirit that makes it possible.

John 3, Acts 2

THE NEW LIFE

"I came that they may have life, and have it abundantly."

(Jn 10:10, RSV)

Words of Life

Day 1:

Throughout the ages, prophets predicted that the day would come when God would give his Spirit freely to men. Those who turned to him and received his Spirit would be changed. They would be new men with a new life.

The Lord God says this.... "I shall pour clean water over you and you will be cleansed.... I shall give you a new heart, and put a new spirit in you; I shall remove the heart of stone from

your bodies and give you a heart of flesh
instead. I shall put my spirit in you.... You shall
be my people and I will be your God."

(adapted from Ezek 36:22–28, JB)

Day 2:

Jesus promised before he died that he would
give his followers the Holy Spirit. The Holy Spirit
will live in you and give you new life. The
promise of Jesus is for everyone. Jesus says:

If you love me you will keep my
commandments.
I shall ask the Father,
and he will give you another Advocate
to be with you for ever,
that Spirit of truth
whom the world can never receive
since it neither sees nor knows him;
but you know him,
because he is with you, he is in you.
I will not leave you orphans.

(Jn 14:15-18, JB)

Day 3:

On the day of Pentecost, Jesus' disciples were gathered together in one room in prayer, and the Holy Spirit, which Jesus promised, came on them. From that moment on, they were changed men.

> *When Pentecost day came round... they were all filled with the Holy Spirit and began to speak in tongues as the Spirit gave them the gift of speech.*
>
> (adapted from Acts 2:1–4, JB)

Day 4:

You can experience the Holy Spirit the same way the first disciples did. Whether you have been a Christian for a while or have never believed in Christ before, you can receive whatever is missing in your experience of the life of the Spirit. What happened to the disciples at Ephesus can happen to you.

> *When they heard this, they were baptized in the name of the Lord Jesus, and the moment Paul had laid hands on them the Holy Spirit came down on them, and they began to speak with tongues and to prophesy. There were about twelve of these men.*
>
> (Acts 19:5–7, JB)

Day 5:

When the Holy Spirit is released in you, you will begin to experience a new kind of life. You will know God in a new way. That new life will grow in you until you become a changed person. Paul describes the result by saying:

The fruit of the Spirit is love, joy, peace, patience, kindness, goodness, faithfulness, gentleness, self-control.

(Gal 5:22–23, RSV)

Day 6:

As you grow in faith in the Holy Spirit in you, you will begin to experience him working in you in new ways so that you can serve others. He will equip you with spiritual gifts, gifts which will give you a new power to do his work. Paul talks about some of these gifts in this way:

The particular way in which the Spirit is given to each person is for a good purpose. One may have the gift of preaching with wisdom given him by the Spirit; another may have the gift of preaching instruction given him by the same Spirit; and another the gift of faith given by the same Spirit; another again the gift of healing through this one Spirit; one, the power of miracles; another, prophecy; another the gift of recognizing spirits; another the gift of tongues and another the ability to interpret them. All these are the work of one and the same Spirit, who distributes different gifts to different people just as he chooses.

(1 Cor 12:7–11, JB)

Day 7:

God gives the Holy Spirit so that we can be joined to the body of Christ (the Church, the Christian community). The new life in the Spirit will allow you to be more closely united with other Christians in the Church and to experience a communion with them in the Spirit. God's word teaches:

So you are no longer aliens or foreign visitors; you are citizens like all the saints, and part of God's household. You are part of a building that has the apostles and prophets for its foundations, and Christ Jesus himself for its main cornerstone. As every structure is aligned on him, all grow into one holy temple in the Lord; and you too, in him, are being built into a house where God lives, in the Spirit.

(Eph 2:19–22, JB)

Study

This week the two chapters we will read are about turning to the Lord in faith and repentance.

John 4, Acts 13

RECEIVING GOD'S GIFT

"If any man is thirsty, let him come to me! Let the man come and drink who believes in me! As scripture says, From his breast shall flow fountains of living water."
(Jn 7:37–38, JB)

Preparing to be baptized in the Spirit

Brother or sister,

This week the Lord himself wants to prepare you. Do not be afraid or worried. Do not ask yourself how you can possibly get ready. Just ask the Lord to prepare you. He loves you, and he will do it.

Let the words of life speak to you. God's word will prepare you.

Do not let Satan confuse you. If you feel confusion or doubt or anxiety come on you, tell Satan to go away. Tell him you belong to Jesus and Jesus is your Lord. Put your faith in God.

God loves you. He wants to give you the fullness of life in the Spirit. He has promised that he will give the Holy Spirit to those who ask. Simply ask in confidence.

Satan will tell you that you do not deserve to be baptized in the Spirit, that you are not worthy of it. And he is right. No one is worthy of it. But God is not going to baptize you in the Spirit because you are worthy of it, he will do it because he loves you. He will do it because Jesus died for you.

Jesus will change your life when you make the commitment to him and are prayed with. You will begin a new life in the Spirit. You can count on it. Simply rely on God's promise.

Do not look for a particular kind of experience. Some people experience a great deal at the moment when they are prayed with, while others experience very little. What you want is the Holy Spirit, not an experience. Once you are in a new relationship with the Holy Spirit, you will experience a new sense of his presence. You will see him work in your life in a new way.

Ask the Lord for the gift of tongues. Tongues is a gift of God, and even if you do not understand fully what it will do for you, trust God that his gifts really are gifts and worth having. If you are unwilling to receive the gift of tongues, you are putting a block on the Lord's work and the Holy Spirit will not be free to work fully in you. Open yourself to all of God's gifts, with no reservations.

Relax. God loves you. Remember that his fatherly love surrounds you. Remember that he sent his Son to save you. Each day entrust your life to his hands.

Read these words often this week. They will help you to prepare to be baptized in the Spirit.

> Our soul awaits the Lord,
> he is our help and shield;
> our hearts rejoice in him,
> we trust in his holy name.
> Lord, let your love rest on us
> as our hope has rested in you.

The commitment to Christ

In the next seminar, you will make a commitment to Christ before being prayed with to be baptized in the Spirit. The leader will ask you three questions, and after you answer them, you will say a prayer expressing a commitment to Christ. Meditate on these questions and on the prayer during this week:

Do you renounce Satan and all wrongdoing?

Do you believe that Jesus is the Son of God, that he died to free us from our sins, and that he rose to bring us new life?

Will you follow Jesus as your Lord?

Lord Jesus Christ, I want to belong to you from now on. I want to be freed from the dominion of darkness and the rule of Satan, and I want to enter into your kingdom and be part of your people. I will turn away from all wrongdoing, and I will avoid everything that leads me to wrongdoing. I ask you to forgive all the sins that I have committed. I offer my life to you, and I promise to obey you as my Lord. I ask you to baptize me in the Holy Spirit and give me the gift of tongues.

Words of Life

Day 1:

God has a new life for you, because he loves you. It is a gift. You cannot earn it or deserve it. God's word says:

> *When the kindness and love of God our savior for mankind were revealed, it was not because he was concerned with any righteous actions we might have done ourselves; it was for no reason except his own compassion that he saved us, by means of the cleansing water of rebirth and by renewing us with the Holy Spirit which he has so generously poured over us through Jesus Christ our savior.*
>
> (Ti 3:4–6, JB)

Day 2:

The new life in the Spirit is a gift, but you have to turn to Jesus to receive it. All those who come to him receive new life abundantly. Jesus says:

> *If any man is thirsty, let him come to me!*
> *Let the man come and drink who believes in me!*
> *As scripture says, From his breast shall flow fountains of living water.*
>
> (Jn 7:37–38, JB)

Day 3:

To turn to Jesus you turn away from everything incompatible with the life he is offering (repentance) and accept the promises he is making (belief and faith). When you turn to Jesus in repentance and faith, he can give new life to you. Jesus says:

> *"The time has come" he said "and the kingdom of God is close at hand. Repent and believe the Good News [the gospel]."*
>
> (Mk 1:15, JB)

Day 4:

This new life is for everyone who will turn to the Lord. The gift of the Holy Spirit is for you. Satan will try to deceive you into thinking that you are someone who cannot be baptized in the Spirit, but the word of God says:

> *You must repent…and every one of you must be baptized in the name of Jesus Christ for the forgiveness of your sins, and you will receive the gift of the Holy Spirit. The promise that was made is for you and your children, and for all those who are far away, for all those whom the Lord our God will call to himself.*
>
> (Acts 2:38–39, JB)

Day 5:

You cannot earn or deserve the gift of the Holy
Spirit, but you do have to put away everything in
your life which is incompatible with the Christian
life. The new life means that you will be holy as
God is holy. God's word says:

> *Do you not know that the unrighteous will not*
> *inherit the kingdom of God? Do not be deceived;*
> *neither the immoral, nor idolaters, nor adulterers,*
> *nor sexual perverts, nor thieves, nor the greedy,*
> *nor drunkards, nor revilers, nor robbers will*
> *inherit the kingdom of God.*
>
> (adapted from 1 Cor 6:9–10, RSV)

Day 6:

Faith means relying on what God has promised.
You know that God can do anything. You know
that he does not lie. Rely on God's promise and
claim them from him as Abraham did, and you
will see him work in a new way in your life. God's
word says:

> *Since God had promised it, Abraham refused*
> *either to deny it or even to doubt it, but drew*
> *strength from faith and gave glory to God,*

convinced that God had power to do what he had promised.

(Rom 4:20–21, JB)

Day 7:

When you turn to the Lord in repentance and faith, all you have to do is ask the Lord for the fullness of life in the Holy Spirit. We know that we can have the Holy Spirit, because God loves us and wants to be as fully united to us as possible. Jesus promises that the Father will give the Holy Spirit to those who ask him.

> *So I say to you: Ask, and it will be given to you.... What father among you would hand his son a stone when he asked for bread? Or hand him a snake instead of a fish?... If you then, who are evil, know how to give your children what is good, how much more will the heavenly Father give the Holy Spirit to those who ask him!*

(Lk 11:9–13, JB)

Study

This week the two chapters we will read are about the life of the Spirit and the power of God in us:

John 14, Acts 8

BAPTIZED IN THE SPIRIT

"To set the mind on the flesh is death, but to set the mind on the Spirit is life and peace."

(Rom 8:6, RSV)

Day One

Last night you were prayed with. Today is a new day. You may feel a new joy, a new peace, a praise of God welling up within you. You may feel doubt, a feeling that you made a fool of yourself last night, a feeling of confusion or depression. You may even feel all of those things at once. But the life of the Spirit is not based on feelings.

Today is the day to begin a new life in faith. If you committed your life to Christ and asked him to baptize you in the Holy Spirit, then you were baptized in the Spirit. You may feel any number of things, but you made a new beginning last night. Now you must live that new beginning in faith.

Consider the facts. When you are baptized in the Spirit, the Holy Spirit is in you in a new way. You are not yet fully controlled by the Holy Spirit, you still have to grow into the life of the Spirit, but he is in you in a new way.

Satan is also concerned with you in a new way. Since you now have more spiritual power, you are more dangerous to him, and he would like to stop you. After Jesus was baptized, he entered into spiritual battle in a new way (Lk 4:1–13). In the same way, now that you have been baptized in the Holy Spirit, you enter into spiritual battle in a new way.

Suppose a friend of yours wanted to get into a certain room, and he came to you and you gave him a key. Now suppose that someone wants to keep your friend from getting into that room. He has the key, and nothing should stop him from entering. But if he can be convinced that he does not really have the key, then he may never use it, and he would not get into the room. Now that you have been baptized in the Spirit, Satan will try to make you think it was not real or that it did not happen to you. That's his number one tactic.

His number two tactic is just the opposite. His number two tactic is to convince you that now that you have the Holy Spirit you are all set. Your problems are gone, you don't need anything or anyone else. He will try to make you think you do not need to pray, you do not need to learn how to live in the Spirit, you do not need the help of other Christians. If you see a train of thought like that starting to go through your mind, beware. You are being built up for a fall.

Have no fear. Simply put your faith in God. Resist all doubts and anxieties. Let the joy and peace and praise of God fill you. In humility begin to learn from God and from your brothers and sisters how to live the life of the Spirit. Remember that you are only a beginner.

Do not let the gift of tongues worry you. If you did not pray in tongues last night, just look for it to happen. It could happen almost anytime. If you said something last night but are not sure whether it was tongues or not, keep on saying it. If it was tongues, it will grow and develop. If it was not tongues, it can turn into tongues. If you did pray in tongues but it sounds like stuttering, keep on doing it. It will grow and develop.

Pray in tongues every day. It will grow in value for you.

You need the Life in the Spirit Seminars now more than you did before. The lessons of the next two weeks are very important. Now that you have been baptized in the Spirit, you need to grow in the life of the Spirit. If you are having any difficulties or are unsure what has happened, Satan will try hard to keep you away from other Christians. Do not let him talk you out of attending the next two seminars.

God loves you. He wants you to live in union with him. Living in the life of the Spirit is very simple: listen to God's word, put your faith in it and obey it. He will lead you.

Words of Life

Day 1:
When you were prayed with yesterday, a change was made in your life. You can count on

Satan to try to confuse you. You can count on God to be with you and to want to lead you to a new life. God's word says:

> Unload all your worries on [God], since he is looking after you. Be calm but vigilant, because your enemy the devil is prowling round like a roaring lion, looking for someone to eat. Stand up to him, strong in faith.

(1 Pet 5:7–9, JB)

Day 2:

The Lord has given you a new power in the Spirit. Make use of it. It may not seem like much at the moment, or it may seem like a lot, but make use of what he has given you, and it will increase. The Lord commends those who are faithful when he says:

> Well done, good and faithful servant; you have shown you can be faithful in small things, I will trust you with greater; come and join in your master's happiness.

(Mt 25:23, JB)

Day 3:

When you live in the Spirit, the Spirit prays in you. Let him pray in you often during the day, sometimes in English, sometimes in the new tongue he has given you. Even if you have only a few syllables in a new tongue or if you are not sure of it, pray in that tongue every day and it will grow. God's word encourages you:

Pray all the time, asking for what you need praying in the Spirit on every possible occasion.
(Eph 6:18, JB)

Day 4:

Learn to set your thoughts on the Lord and on the things of the Spirit. Think about the Lord. Meditate on the words of life he speaks. Understand how to live his life. If God's truth forms your mind, you will find life and peace. God's word promises you:

To set the mind on the flesh is death, but to set the mind on the Spirit is life and peace.
(Rom 8:6, RSV)

Day 5:

The Lord wants you to have spiritual gifts, because he wants to give you power to serve him in an effective way. But he wants you to know that the aim of the Christian life is to love

God and to love one another. That must be the center of your concern. God's word says:

> *Make love your aim, and earnestly desire the spiritual gifts.*
>
> (1 Cor 14:1a, RSV)

Day 6:

How can you tell if you are a spiritual person? Frequently people have the idea that we are spiritual if we have many spiritual gifts. But spiritual gifts are not a good measure of how spiritual we are. You can tell if you are a spiritual person by how much the fruit of the Spirit (love, joy, peace and patience, kindness, generosity, faithfulness, gentleness, self-control) characterizes your life. Paul warns us as he speaks to the Corinthians:

> *Brothers, I myself was unable to speak to you as people of the spirit: I treated you as sensual men, still infants in Christ. What I fed you with was milk, not solid food, for you were not ready for it; and indeed, you are still not ready for it since you are still unspiritual. Isn't that obvious from all the jealousy and wrangling that there is among you?*
>
> (1 Cor 3:1–3, JB)

Day 7:

God wants us to live with him in heaven. The difficulties we face on earth are small compared with the glory of heaven. The gift of the Spirit is simply the first installment, a pledge of what is to come. God promises you:

> *Yes, the troubles which are soon over, though they weigh little, train us for the carrying of a weight of eternal glory which is out of all proportion to them.... For we know that when the tent that we live in on earth is folded up, there is a house built by God for us, an everlasting home not made by human hands, in the heavens.... This is the purpose for which God made us, and he has given us the pledge of the Spirit.*

> (2 Cor 4:16; 5:1, 5, JB)

Study

This week the two chapters we will read are about growing in our union with Christ and in our life in the Spirit.

John 15, Galatians 5

GROWTH

"I am the vine, you are the branches. Whoever remains in me, with me in him, bears fruit in plenty; for cut off from me you can do nothing."

(Jn 15:5, JB)

Not to go forward is to go backward. When we begin a new life, we have to grow, or we will always be stunted and incomplete. You have been given a new life, now you must grow to maturity in it.

Being baptized in the Spirit is only a beginning. It is a first step. It should not be the spiritual high point of your life. It should be the low point—from this time onward. The Lord wants it to be the beginning of a better and better life.

You have a seed of new life in you. With the right soil and the right care a seed will grow naturally. Learn how to care for it, and have no fear; it will grow.

The Wheel

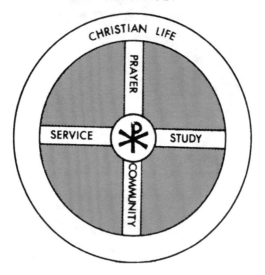

The wheel represents your life as a Christian.

The rim of the wheel represents your daily life. As the rim revolves around the hub, you move forward.

The hub of the wheel is Christ. The hub of the wheel is the source of power and direction for the whole wheel. Christ is the source of power and direction for your life.

Spokes transmit the power and direction from the hub to the rim. As long as the rim is in contact with the hub through the spokes, it can move forward. Some spokes for your Christian life are:

> prayer
> study (of God's word)
> community (life shared with other Christians)
> service

Growth comes from Christ, who gives you a new life. But you need to do those things which will keep you in contact with him.

> pray every day
> study God's word regularly
> meet with other Christians
>   for prayer and sharing regularly
> find a means of Christian service,
>   especially find a way to share the
>   life you have been given

Words of Life

Day 1:

Jesus has given you a new life through the Holy Spirit. The life of the Holy Spirit in you is not like a pool of water that you have to guard carefully or it will turn dry. It is like a flowing spring that will grow in you unless you do something to stop it up. Jesus promises you:

> *Anyone who drinks the water that I shall give*
> *will never be thirsty again:*
> *the water that I shall give*
> *will turn into a spring inside him, welling up to*
> *eternal life.*

(Jn 4:14, JB)

Day 2:

Your life is in Christ; it comes from Christ. If you stay firmly joined to him, it will grow and bear fruit. If you let yourself be separated from him, it will wither away. Jesus says:

> *I am the vine,*
> *you are the branches.*
> *Whoever remains in me, with me in him,*
> *bears fruit in plenty;*
> *for cut off from me you can do nothing.*

Anyone who does not remain in me
is like a branch that has been thrown away
—he withers.

(Jn 15:5–6, JB)

Day 3:

Jesus has given you a new self, a new way of life that is more spiritual, happier and better than the old. But you must actively put away your old self so that you might experience this new life. God's word urges you:

You must give up your old way of life; you must put aside your old self, which gets corrupted by following illusory desires. Your minds must be renewed by a spiritual revolution so that you can put on the new self that has been created in God's way, in the goodness and holiness of the truth.

(Eph 4:22–23, JB)

Day 4:

In order to keep in contact with God who is our source of life, you should pray. Jesus prayed. Although he was the son of God, although he was very busy, he knew he had to pray. You too have to pray if you wish to stay alive spiritually. Imitate Jesus.

> *[Jesus'] reputation continued to grow, and large crowds would gather to hear him and to have their sickness cured, but he would always go off to some place where he could be alone and pray.*
>
> (Lk 5:15–16, JB)

Day 5:

In order to grow in the life of the Spirit, you need to know what God teaches. The Scriptures are the word of God, and they contain words of life. Read them and meditate on them faithfully and you will grow. God's word says:

> *From the holy scriptures you can learn the wisdom that leads to salvation through faith in Christ Jesus. All scripture is inspired by God and can profitably be used for teaching, for refuting error, for guiding people's lives and teaching them to be holy.*
>
> (adapted from 2 Tim 3:15–17, JB)

Day 6:

The Christian life is not an individualistic life. By himself, a Christian is incomplete. The gift of the Spirit led the first Christians to join together and to form a community in which they helped one another to grow. Be faithful to the Church and to meeting with the Christians who have helped you find new life in the Spirit. Imitate the Christians on the day of Pentecost.

> *That very day about three thousand were added to their number. These remained faithful to the teaching of the apostles, to the brotherhood, to the breaking of bread, and to the prayers.... The faithful all lived together and owned everything in common.... They shared their food gladly and generously; they praised God and were looked up to by everyone. Day by day the Lord added to their community those destined to be saved.*
>
> (Acts 2:41–47, JB)

Day 7:

If you love other people, you will want to share with them the best thing you have—the Lord. Share what you have found with wisdom, following the leading of the Spirit. God's word says:

> *Be tactful with those who are not Christians and be sure that you make the best use of your time with them. Talk to them agreeably and with*

a flavor of wit, and try to fit your answers to the
needs of each one.

(Col 4:5–6, JB)

Study

This week the two chapters we will read are about continuing faithfully in our life with Jesus and being changed into being like him:

John 17, Philippians 3

TRANSFORMATION IN CHRIST

"Not that I have already obtained this or am already perfect; but I press on to make it my own, because Christ Jesus has made me his own."

(Phil 3:12, RSV)

Words of Life

Day 1:

The Holy Spirit is at work in you. He wants to change you, to give you a better life, to make you holier. You can rely on him and his work in your life. Jesus did not leave you on your own to work things out. God's word promises:

> *It is God, for his own loving purpose, who puts both the will and the action into you.*
>
> (Phil 2:13, JB)

Day 2:

Never let this truth dim in your mind: there is nothing as worthwhile as knowing Christ and belonging to him. Your greatest treasure is the life you have in Christ. Give up everything to keep that life and grow in it. God's word says:

> *I believe nothing can happen that will outweigh the supreme advantage of knowing Christ Jesus my Lord. For him I have accepted the loss of everything, and I look on everything as so much rubbish if only I can have Christ and be given a place in him.*
>
> (Phil 3:8–9, JB)

Day 3:

Sometimes you will run into trials. Friends will misunderstand you, your family may try to make you give up, you will experience doubts, fears, confusion. But all these things can be means of growth and change for the better if you go through them in faith. God's word promises:

My brothers, you will always have your trials,
but when they come try to treat them as a
happy privilege; you understand that your faith
is only put to the test to make you patient, but
patience too is to have its practical results so
that you will become fully-developed, complete,
with nothing missing.

(Jas 1:2–4, JB)

Day 4:

God is with you. Never forget that. He loves you
and is with you and will never desert you. No
matter what trial you have to face, the LORD
WHO LOVES YOU IS WITH YOU. God's word
promises:

The trials that you have had to bear are no more
than people normally have. You can trust God not
to let you be tried beyond your strength, and with
any trial he will give you a way out of it and the
strength to bear it.

(1 Cor 10:13, JB)

Day 5:

If you are faithful to God and love him,
everything will work out to your good. There is
nothing that will happen to you that will not be a

source of deeper and better life to you. The Lord brings good out of evil. His word promises:

> *We know that by turning everything to their good God co-operates with all those who love him, with all those he has called according to his purpose.*
>
> (Rom 8:28, JB)

Day 6:

You cannot be fully united to Christ without being united to the body of Christ. If you love Christ, love his body, love those who belong to him. If you want to belong to Christ, join yourself to his body, stay close to other Christians. God's word says:

> *Just as each of our bodies that has several parts and each part has a separate function, so all of us, in union with Christ, form one body, and as parts of it we belong to each other.*
>
> (Rom 12:4–5, JB)

Day 7:

Jesus will work in your life through the Church and through other Christians. He wants you to take a care for the life of the Christian community and for helping other Christians. Be faithful to the meetings of the Christians who have helped you find new life in the Spirit. God's word says:

> *Let us be concerned for each other, to stir a response in love and good works. Do not stray away from the meetings of the community, as some do, but encourage each other to go.*
>
> (Heb 10:24–25, JB)

Study
This week the two chapters we will read are about the resurrection of Jesus and our resurrection.

John 20, Revelation 21

Brother or sister,

If you had been given a million dollars, you would guard it very carefully. You have been given something of much more value. Guard it very, very carefully. It is worth giving your life for.

Jesus told a story about a merchant in search of fine pearls. He said, "Again, the kingdom of heaven is like a merchant looking for fine pearls; when he finds one of great value he goes and sells everything he owns and buys it" (Mt 13:45–46, JB). The pearl of great value is the kingdom of God; it is life lived under the reign of God; it is God himself. Give up anything for this pearl.

Jesus says to you, "Do not let your hearts be troubled. Trust in God still, and trust in me" (Jn 14:1). Have no fear, God is with you, and he loves you. He will care for you. With him in you nothing can overcome you.

All your problems have not yet been solved. You are not yet perfect. But you have the way, the truth and the life. You are on the path to eternal glory.

After saying this, what can we add? With God on our side who can be against us? Since God did not spare his own Son, but gave him up to benefit us all, we may be certain, after such a gift, that he will not refuse anything he can give. Could anyone accuse those that God has chosen? When God acquits, could anyone condemn? Could Christ Jesus? No! He not only died for us—he rose from the dead, and there at God's right hand he stands and pleads for us.

Nothing therefore can come between us and the love of Christ, even if we are troubled or worried, or being persecuted, or lacking food or clothes, or being threatened or even attacked.… These are the trials through which we triumph, by the power of him who loved us.

For I am certain of this: neither death nor life, no angel, no prince, nothing that exists, nothing still to come, not any power, or height or depth, nor any created thing, can ever come between us and the love of God made visible in Christ Jesus our Lord.

(Rom 8:31–39, JB)

Commonly Used Prayers

Our father *in heaven,*
Hallowed be your name,
Your kingdom come,
Your will be done,
    on earth as it is in heaven.
Give us this day our daily bread.
And forgive us our trespasses,
    as we forgive those
    who trespass against us;
And lead us not into temptation,
    but deliver us from evil.

Glory be *to the Father,*
    and to the Son,
    and to the Holy Spirit,
As it was in the beginning,
    is now and ever shall be,
    world without end. Amen.

Come, Holy Spirit, *fill the hearts of your faithful, and enkindle in them the fire of your love.*

V. Send forth your Spirit, and they shall be created.

R. And you shall renew the face of the earth.

Let us pray.

O God, who by the light of the Holy Spirit, did instruct the hearts of your faithful, grant that by that same Holy Spirit, we may be truly wise, and ever rejoice in his consolation, through Christ our Lord, Amen.

Come, Holy Ghost, *creator blest,*
and in our hearts take up thy rest.
Come with thy grace, and heavenly aid,
to fill the hearts which thou hast made,
to fill the hearts which thou hast made.

O comforter, to thee we cry,
thou heavenly gift of God most high.
Thou font of life and fire of love,
and sweet anointing from above,
and sweet anointing from above.

Praise be to thee, Father and Son
and Holy Spirit with them one.

And may the Son on us bestow
   the gifts that from the Spirit flow,
   the gifts that from the Spirit flow.

I believe *in God the Father Almighty,*
   Creator of heaven and earth.
And in Jesus Christ his only Son, our Lord,
Who was conceived by the Holy Spirit,
   born of the Virgin Mary,
   suffered under Pontius Pilate,
   was crucified, died and was buried.
He descended into hell
   and on the third day he rose again from the dead.
He ascended into heaven
   and is seated at the right hand of God
   the Father almighty.
From there he shall come to judge
   the living and the dead.
I believe in the Holy Spirit, the holy Catholic Church,
   the communion of saints, the forgiveness of sins,
   the resurrection of the body, and life ever
   lasting. Amen.